THE NO MORE
BULLYING
BOOK FOR KIDS

THE NO MORE BULLYING
BOOK FOR KIDS

BECOME STRONG, HAPPY, AND BULLY-PROOF

Vanessa Green Allen, M.Ed., NBCT

ROCKRIDGE
PRESS

Illustrations © Emmeline Pidgen, 2018
Author photo by Tarsha Burroughs

ISBN: Print 978-1-64152-071-3 | eBook 978-1-64152-072-0

This book is affectionately dedicated with love to my mother, Victoria Burney Green. You are an angel in heaven and a sweet memory in my heart.

CONTENTS

LETTER TO ADULTS

To parents, teachers, school counselors, administrators, and other mentors: Thank you for choosing this resource to better understand the effects of bullying and to spark conversations with the children in your life. Bullying can take a tremendous toll on children both physically and emotionally and have damaging long-term effects. For these reasons, it's important to take the time with kids to discuss what it really is and what they can do when faced with it.

These are the goals of *The No More Bullying Book for Kids*:

Help children identify what bullying really is. This includes learning about the different types of bullying, as well as the differences between bullying and just being mean. Understanding this is crucial, so children don't get into the habit of calling every mean or rude kid a bully. It's also important for you to know the difference, because as an adult in their lives, you have the power to influence interventions that can help change bullying behaviors.

Help children know what to do when they are the target of bullying. This includes helping them think about what to say to bullies, when to ignore them, and how to carry themselves with confidence.

Additionally, they will learn what to do when they witness bullying as bystanders.

Help children develop skills to increase their resilience. This includes encouraging them to have a positive attitude and helping them learn how to become problem solvers.

Encourage children to talk with the supportive adults in their lives. This is a very important goal. Many children are afraid to tell an adult about bullying and instead try to handle it themselves while suffering in silence. This book will give them a clear idea of when to ask for help, and of which things should be shared with an adult right away.

You can help the children in your life get the most out of this book by reading it with them and making sure they understand the information, tips, and strategies. Talk through the discussion questions included throughout the book, and encourage children to make connections with their own experiences. I also encourage you to assist them with using the pact at the end of the book. It can work in school, team, or club settings and even between small groups of friends. By doing all these things and letting them know you're there for them, you will help bring bullying out into the light for open discussion and equip children with tools to face social challenges with a plan and with confidence.

INTRODUCTION

Dear Reader,

My name is Vanessa Allen and I am a school counselor in North Carolina. I have helped many children solve problems, overcome challenges, and become stronger, and I wrote this book so that you can, too!

You probably know someone who has been bullied, or you may have been bullied yourself. You are not alone. Many children everywhere deal with bullying in some form every day. It can make you feel helpless and lonely, and you may think there is nothing you can do to make it go away. Although bullying is very common in schools and neighborhoods, you DO have the power to overcome it when you have the right tools. With its many stories, tips, and strategies, *The No More Bullying Book for Kids* will give you the information and tools you need to empower yourself.

This book begins by helping you recognize bullying behaviors. This doesn't mean recognizing what a bully looks like—bullies all look different. It means noticing and recognizing the things they do. You will learn what bullying really is and the different types of bullying. You will also get a better understanding of the differences between bullying and teasing.

Next, you will learn how to stand up to bullying with words and actions that work. You'll understand when to ask adults for help for yourself and others. You will learn how you can help bullies change their behavior. You'll also get a better understanding of what cyberbullying is and learn ways to defend yourself and others online.

Finally, you will learn what it means to be *resilient* (that means "tough") and the different steps you can take toward making yourself bully-proof. You'll even have a special agreement, called a *pact*, that you can make at the end with your friends or classmates.

Throughout this book, you'll find sections that will get you thinking about bullying and how to handle different situations. My quick tips can help you find your way through tough situations. I've also included lots of scenarios and real-life stories with questions for you to answer and activities to help test your knowledge of what you've learned. This book is designed to be shared—please read and talk about these sections with the adults and friends in your life.

So, now it's time to read, gather your tools, and learn how to live a bully-free life. You've got supporters behind you—that's why you have this book, right? So let's go!

Sincerely,
Vanessa Allen

ONE

Recognize Bullying

WHAT IS BULLYING?

Have you ever been bullied? Let's think about it. The word *bullied* is often used to describe different things, like being called names, being picked on, and being laughed at or talked about by other kids. Other bullying behaviors include being punched, kicked, or threatened. Not every bad behavior is bullying, though. Some kids may do and say mean things to you because they are just being rude or having a bad day and making poor decisions. These choices aren't nice, but they don't make those kids bullies. So, how DO you know when it is really bullying? Here's a definition:

Bullying is a repeated pattern of aggressive behavior where someone in a position of power intentionally seeks to hurt others physically, verbally, or emotionally.

An important word in this definition is repeated. When something is repeated, it happens more than one time. So, a situation is considered "bullying" when the hurtful actions keep happening to you over and over again. A person who repeats the same sort of behavior to hurt more than one person can also be considered a bully.

QUICK TIP: Although bullying is repeated behavior, there are times when you should report a single action to a trusted adult right away. Trusted adults can include your parents, teachers, school counselors, principals, and coaches. They can also include other family members, like aunts, uncles, and grandparents.

What should you report immediately?

- If someone hurts you or someone else physically
- If someone threatens to hurt you or someone else
- If someone threatens you or someone else with a weapon or threatens to use a weapon to hurt you

WHY DO KIDS BULLY?

What makes a kid bully someone else? Although every situation is different, here are a few reasons why:

Learned behavior: Some kids witness bullying behaviors every day. They may see parents or siblings treat others badly and begin to copy that behavior. They could also be the targets of bullying themselves and mistreat others as a result.

Power and control: Some kids like to use their power in order to be in control. Power can come from height, size, or popularity. The attention someone gets from being popular can make them want to "run the show."

Lack of empathy: Empathy is the ability to imagine how someone else is feeling; it's also known as "putting yourself in someone else's shoes." Empathy can be learned, but if kids don't have empathy, they won't think about how their actions make others feel.

Low self-concept: Self-concept is what a person believes about himself or herself. Kids who have a low self-concept may use bullying as a way to give themselves a boost. These kinds of kids often feel better when they make others feel bad.

Ignorance about differences: Many kids are picked on because they look, act, or live differently from others. For example, a bully may not be educated or understand about kids with special needs or different religions and may focus attention on those differences to bring others down.

 QUICK TIP: A bully can be a boy or girl, big or tall, short or thin—anyone can be a bully!

REAL-LIFE STORY

Carlos is a smart, hardworking student in sixth grade. Because he has spoken Spanish all of his life, he goes to a special class each day with a teacher who helps him learn and understand English. One day, after school on the bus, Carlos sits with a Spanish-speaking friend and they begin to talk about their day in their native language. Kevin, who is seated behind them, yells, "You're in America! Speak English!" As he laughs, a few students close by laugh along with him. Carlos is embarrassed and hurt by Kevin's mean words. The next day at lunch, as Carlos is about to put his tray on a table and sit down, Kevin rushes over and pushes Carlos out of the way, knocking his pizza to the floor and taking his seat. Kevin says, "Only people who speak English can sit at this table." As Carlos bends down to pick up his lunch from the floor, Kevin's friend Emily snaps a picture of Carlos on her cell phone. Later that day in class, laughter erupts at Kevin's table as he and Emily look at her cell phone. As Kevin looks over at Carlos, he says to Emily, "Hey, send that picture to me. I know just where to post it!"

LET'S DISCUSS: How do all the events in Carlos's story come together to create a bullying situation?

TYPES OF BULLYING

Bullying can happen physically, verbally, or emotionally. It can also happen on the Internet. Let's explore these three main types of bullying, and the special case of cyberbullying.

PHYSICAL BULLYING

When most kids describe bullying, they usually say it is when a person hits, kicks, punches, or hurts another person in some way. These kinds of behaviors are **physical bullying**. Physical bullying is the act of hurting a person's body, destroying their personal property, or taking things that belong to them without their permission. Being shoved in a locker or having lunch money stolen are typical examples of physical bullying—those are also the types of bullying behaviors we usually see on television. Let's read an example.

QUICK TIP: Although you may be tempted to fight back physically, resist the urge (see Defending Yourself, page 31). Speaking your mind if you feel comfortable, walking away, and getting help from an adult are the safest, smartest ways to deal with physical bullying so no one gets hurt.

IMAGINE THIS: You ride the
bus to school each day, and
you all have assigned seats.
The kid who sits behind you
is always kicking the back
of your seat just to annoy
you. One day, you get up the
nerve to speak up and ask her
to stop, but that just fuels the fire.

Next, instead of kicking the seat, she starts
reaching over the seat, hitting you on the head and daring you
to "tell." One day, she reaches across and grabs your notepad.
When you try to get it back, she tosses it out the window.

Can you see how these events describe physical bullying?

Physical bullying can include someone tripping you as you
walk down the aisle on the bus or cornering you in the school
bathroom and shoving you against a wall. No matter what, it
can be painful and embarrassing.

VERBAL BULLYING

Not all people who bully use their fists. Some use name-calling
and putting others down as their weapons. These behaviors
are examples of **verbal bullying**. Verbal bullying is when a
person uses hurtful words to try to tear down another person's
self-esteem and self-worth. This type of bullying actually
happens more often than physical bullying, and it can be just
as harmful. Have you ever heard a person put someone down
with their words? Read on for an example.

IMAGINE THIS: One day at school, the teacher asks students to take turns reading parts of the science activity aloud. You have a hard time with reading and you are sure that Mark, who sits at your table, will call you names like he always does when the teacher calls on you to read. Before you know it, you hear your name being called to read the next paragraph. As you attempt to read the words, stumbling over a couple of difficult ones, you hear Mark mumble under his breath, "Read it already! You're so dumb!"

Do you see how hurtful words can bring a person down?

Being called names over and over, or being made to feel worthless and unimportant, is really bullying—and it can really hurt. Even though verbal bullying doesn't involve touching, it can stick around in the heart and mind of the bullied person for a long time.

EMOTIONAL BULLYING

Bullying behaviors can hurt others' feelings and cause a lot of pain. Some bullying behaviors are even designed to sabotage (or damage) a person or make them feel ignored and excluded. This is called **emotional bullying**. Emotional bullying is when a person makes another feel afraid or sad in order to get his or her way. It can involve spreading rumors and gossip to destroy the person's friendships and social life or leaving them out on purpose. Check out the following example.

IMAGINE THIS: Diane is a new friend you've made this school year. Madison is a popular girl in your school who has invited you to hang out with her sometimes, but she never invites Diane. One day you and Diane plan to eat lunch together. Madison tells you that Diane is "lame" and invites you to eat lunch with her instead. She says she'll stop inviting you if you don't cancel with Diane. So you do what Madison says. The next day, Madison tells you to do the same thing, but you tell her that Diane will feel bad if you keep canceling on her. This time, Madison threatens to tell people a personal and embarrassing story you told her last week. You don't want to let Diane down, but you really don't want anyone to know about your personal business.

Can you see how this adds up to emotional bullying?

Emotional bullying can also include putting someone down because they are different. Think of something that makes you unique. Now imagine if you were always excluded or made fun of because of it. As you can imagine, it would really hurt. If emotional bullying happens for long enough, targets can become very sad and depressed, so it's important to put a stop to this bullying behavior.

CYBERBULLYING

More than ever before, kids have access to computers and other technology on a daily basis. Because of that, along with the three types of bullying, it's important to learn about bullying that happens online. **Cyberbullying** is bullying that happens electronically using the Internet on devices like cell phones, tablets, and computers. Cyberbullying can involve verbal bullying when mean and hurtful things are said, and emotional bullying when rumors and gossip are spread. Physical bullying can also happen when the target's private online information is hacked or destroyed. Technology and social media can be very useful tools for life and school, but they can also allow bullying to occur with just the click of a mouse or the tap of a screen.

IMAGINE THIS: It's lunchtime, and Kayla asks to use your phone again; this time, to call her brother. Your mom told you not to let anyone use your phone unless it's an emergency. You tell Kayla she can't, but she grabs it from you anyway, as she usually does. When her brother doesn't answer the phone, she hangs up and begins scrolling through your text messages. She selects your friend Daryl's name and sends him a text that says, "U should cut ur hair. U look like a girl." She giggles as she hands the phone back to you. You quickly look to see what she did, only to see a text from Daryl pop up on your screen that says, "I thought you were my friend."

Is there more than one target here?

Cyberbullying occurs when people use social media sites, text messages, and chat rooms to post negative and hurtful things about a person. It can also happen when someone pretends to be someone else while sending mean messages or spreading rumors. Once something is released online, it can go anywhere the recipient decides to send it. When the information is hurtful or threatening, the results can be widespread and very damaging.

REAL-LIFE STORY

Megan is a friendly fifth grader. She often gets her clothes second-hand, but she's always been happy with how she looks each day. One day, a group of girls at school who usually ignore Megan ask her if she wants to play during recess. Megan is surprised but excited to get to know the girls. This group of girls is all about fashion—they always dress very stylishly. Megan has often wished she could afford some of the clothes she sees them wear. This particular day, they decide to pretend they're models so they can post pictures of themselves in their cute outfits. Megan isn't so sure about her outfit, but the girls insist she looks fine for a picture. One girl, Cami, says she will make a collage of all four pictures and post it on her social media to see how many likes they will get. Megan can't wait. They each take a picture using Cami's phone, and Cami promises to have the collage up before bedtime. That night, Megan asks if she can use her mom's cell phone to pull up the site and see her picture. When she finds it, she is shocked and saddened. Her picture is singled out on the right side of the collage with the label "What NOT to Wear."

LET'S DISCUSS: Unkind, right? Which of the types of bullying would you use to describe Megan's story, and why?

WHAT MAKES BULLYING DIFFERENT?

It's important to remember that not every kid who says or does something mean is a bully. Some kids tease or are rude and mean to others. Even though these behaviors can be hurtful, unless they are happening over and over again, it's not considered bullying. Let's look at how bullying is different from teasing, being rude, and being mean, and learn some ways to deal with all these behaviors.

TEASING

Teasing is when a person playfully makes fun of someone else. People tease each other all the time. In fact, you've most likely teased someone before without meaning to hurt his or her feelings. Teasing usually happens among family and friends, but sometimes kids will tease just to get a reaction from you.

So, how do you know it's teasing? Here's an example:

Tara and Jason enjoy hanging out at school and often sit together at lunch. One day, a few of Jason's friends walk by the table and ask Jason if he wants to sit with them. He says, "No thanks. I'll catch you guys later." His friend Brandon says, "He's too busy making googly eyes at his *girlfriend*."

Teasing is different from bullying
because it is not meant to hurt.

Sometimes when people tease you, it may make you upset and you won't think it's funny at all. When teasing is playful, the person teasing will stop if it makes you upset. With bullying, the words or comments are intended to be hurtful, and the behavior doesn't stop when the target gets upset. The bully is usually not someone the person being bullied is close to.

 TALK ABOUT IT: When is teasing okay? What's the difference between harmless teasing and hurtful teasing?

BEING RUDE

There are times when people are just being rude. Many people who behave in a rude way are acting selfishly and not thinking about others. It may frustrate you or even hurt your feelings, but this does not count as bullying. Being rude means a person is being impolite and not using good manners. Someone may bump into you while cutting in front of you in line. Although his actions might upset you, he is not being a bully; he is just being rude. Here is another example of someone being rude:

Evelyn is talking to Jenny after class. Right in the middle of her conversation, Heather walks over and begins talking to Jenny about a movie she saw without saying "excuse me" to Evelyn or even looking her way.

Being rude is different from bullying. Most people who are rude are usually thinking only about themselves and what they want at that time.

Some people may be rude by accident because they are being thoughtless or having a bad day. Others may be rude over and over again, but it rarely has anything to do with you. Unlike a bully, their goal is not to hurt you—it's to get what they want when they want it.

TALK ABOUT IT: What's an effective and respectful way to respond to someone who's being rude to you?

BEING MEAN

There are days when some kids just wake up "on the wrong side of the bed"—that is, grouchy. When that happens, they may purposely say and do hurtful things and upset other kids they come in contact with. However, this doesn't make them bullies. They're just being mean and thoughtless. Can you think of a time when someone you know did or said something mean and it surprised you a little because he or she doesn't usually do or say things like that? You may have thought to yourself, *What is going on with him?* or *Wow, she is having a bad day.* You wouldn't label that person a bully, though, right? Here is an example:

Lilly runs over to the lunch line and accidentally bumps into Alex, making him drop his tray of food on the floor. She immediately apologizes, but Alex calls her a mean name and rolls his eyes at her. He then turns and heads back to the lunch line for another tray.

Being mean is different from bullying. Sometimes people don't use good judgment and don't behave very nicely.

When someone is mean to you, it can hurt your feelings or even make you feel angry. Just remember that meanness doesn't always equal bullying, unless the same person is mistreating you or hurting your feelings repeatedly.

 TALK ABOUT IT: Can you think of a time when you thought someone was being a bully, but now you realize they were just being mean? How do you know?

HOW TO DEAL WITH HURTFUL BEHAVIOR

Bullying is different from the examples of teasing, being rude, or being mean that we just discussed. Here are a few simple ways to deal with hurtful behaviors that are NOT bullying:

1. Tell the person how you feel and how you'd like to see the behavior change. For example: *Ben, I feel frustrated when you won't share the markers with me. Can I use the ones you aren't using?*

2. Walk away from the situation without talking to the kid who's being rude or mean.

3. Try not to appear upset when being teased. Stay cool, and make a joke or laugh about it.

4. Ignore the behavior. Act as if the person never said a word.

5. Use a quick one-line response the other kid won't expect, such as "So?" or "Thanks for telling me."

RECOGNIZING BULLYING

Read each of the following scenarios and decide which type of behavior they describe. Is it physical bullying, verbal bullying, emotional bullying, cyberbullying, or teasing? Why?

1. Liam has been bothering Steve for days, and this morning is no different. As Steve gets on the bus and heads back to his seat, Liam sticks his foot into the aisle, causing Steve to trip and fall forward onto the floor. Is this bullying?

2. Hunter is the shortest in the group of guys he hangs out with. One day, they are all at Tim's house, about to eat a snack in the kitchen. As they go to sit down, Tim says, "Hey! Wait a minute, Hunter. Let me get a booster seat for you." The guys laugh. Is this bullying?

3. Samantha can barely stand it when Eric is around. He asks her questions like, "Are you a girl or a boy?" "Why do you dress like that?" "You should let your hair grow longer. You look like a boy." "You know you're a girl, right?" Samantha had always felt good about herself. Now she has begun to wonder, *Is something wrong with me?* Is Eric bullying?

4. Mike looks for ways to embarrass Jordan almost every day in class. Today, he watches Jordan walk away from his computer and ask to go to the bathroom. When no one is paying attention, Mike goes to Jordan's computer and sends an inappropriate message to the online classroom

chat, which appears to come from Jordan. Someone reports Jordan before he is even able to return to the classroom. Is Mike bullying?

5. Mrs. Johnson asks the class for volunteers to come to the front as a visual for the word *curly*. When Anita raises her hand, Sharon says, "Mrs. Johnson wants *real* hair . . . *real* curls." Several students laugh as Anita gives Sharon a look. Is this bullying?

6. For the third day in a row, Linda attempts to join a group of girls from her class in the lunchroom. As usual, Patty tells her the seat is saved for someone else. Linda doesn't understand. She used to sit with them all the time. As the other girls giggle, Linda finds somewhere else to sit, all alone. Is this bullying?

ANSWERS

1. Yes, it is physical bullying. Physical bullying causes someone to get hurt, and Liam made Steve trip and fall.

2. No, it is teasing. Although the joke is on Hunter, he is friends with Tim. He knows the comment was made just to get a laugh, not to bully.

3. Yes, it is verbal bullying. Eric is saying insulting things to Samantha and making her feel as though something is wrong with just being herself.

4. Yes, it is cyberbullying. Cyberbullying happens on mobile devices and computers. Mike pretended to be Jordan in a chat room and posted an inappropriate message to the class.

5. No, it is teasing. Although it wasn't nice and Anita may be a little embarrassed, this was one random comment by a student in the class.

6. Yes, it is emotional bullying. Emotional bullying can make a person feel isolated and excluded. This group of girls has been repeatedly leaving Linda out on purpose, which causes Linda to feel sad and lonely.

TWO

Stop Bullies

STAND UP TO A BULLY

Now that you know how to recognize bullying, you can make a plan for standing up to bullies. The most important thing to know is that a person who bullies usually wants an easy target, not a person who will calmly stand up to them. Having a plan will make it easier to stay one step ahead.

STAND UP WITH WORDS

One way to stand up to a bully is to use your words. Knowing how to use your words can throw a bully off their game and off your track. Here are a few suggestions:

- Say "no" firmly if the bully is trying to make you do something you don't want to do.

- Agree with what the bully says. It's the last thing the bully will expect.

- Talk about an entirely different subject.

- If all else fails, and you feel physically threatened, alert those nearby and yell "LEAVE ME ALONE!"

To show how to use this strategy to your advantage, here are a few examples:

Gabriel pinches and harasses you on the bus every day so you will let him copy your answers for the math homework, and he always gets his way. In class during math, he tries to do the same thing when the teacher isn't looking.

You could say:

- "No. I'm not giving you the answers."
- "I wonder what's for lunch today."
- "DON'T TOUCH ME!" or "STOP ASKING TO SEE MY PAPER!" (Then, let the teacher take it from there.)

Monica and Lisa have planned a mean prank to play on Jon and they ask you to participate. You think it's really mean and say you don't want to do it. As usual, they threaten to stop hanging out with you if you don't do what they say.

You could say:

- "I guess I'll have to find some new friends."
- "No. I'm not going to treat him that way."
- "You should totally stop hanging out with me, then."

One day, you forget to brush your teeth before school, and a few people can tell. Matthew has been calling you "poop breath" ever since. Today, when you walk into the classroom, Matthew says, "Hey, guys! Here comes poop breath. Watch out!"

You could say:

- "Yep, it's me! I guess you guys better plug your noses."
- "That's so funny, Matthew. Tell me another one!"
- "Ooookay . . . So, what's our morning assignment?"

Bullies want to be in control. When you begin to speak up, they're more likely to leave you alone. Stand up with your words so the bully will stand down.

QUICK TIP: When standing up to a bully with words, do your best to remain respectful. Don't become a bully yourself. (You're better than that.)

STAND UP WITH ACTIONS

Another way to stop a bully is to stand up with your actions. Using body language and other nonverbal actions the right way can be a big help. These are simple and nonviolent steps you can take that will make the bully rethink choosing you as a target. Let's explore how to stand up for yourself by ignoring the bully, showing confidence, and using nonviolent responses to bullying.

Ignore a Bully

Learning to ignore a person who bullies is one way to stand up with your actions. Here are five tips that can help you succeed with this strategy:

1. Walk away without a response. Regardless of what that person says or does, walk away from the situation. If a bully decides to follow you, keep walking and let them follow you—straight to a helpful adult.

2. Don't react. Don't make a face, don't cry—just act as if nothing is being said or done.

3. If the bullying comes in the form of a mean text or e-mail, don't respond. If it's threatening, show an adult.

4. Distract yourself. Open a book, put your earbuds in and listen to music, begin a conversation with a friend, or focus on your classwork if you're at school.

5. Avoid the places where you are likely to see the person.

Ignoring may work for some situations like verbal bullying, but it may not work in other situations. If it doesn't, look to the other options to choose a more effective response.

 TALK ABOUT IT: Why do you think ignoring a bully doesn't always work? In this case, what could you do instead?

Look Confident, Feel Confident

A little confidence can go a long way. When you appear confident and have confidence on the inside, you are less likely to be the target of bullying.

In order to look confident, remember these five tips:

1. Stand tall with your shoulders back.

2. Keep your chin up, looking straight ahead.

3. Use eye contact when speaking to others.

4. Talk with a strong voice so you are heard and understood.

5. Walk with pride, knowing you've got what it takes.

Looking confident is a great start, but it's also important to feel confident. A bully saying a mean thing doesn't make it true. Value yourself and know that you deserve respect. Think positive thoughts about yourself and focus on your strengths. Everyone is good at something. Accept yourself for who you are, and don't ever change who you are to please anyone—especially someone who acts like a bully. Finally, focus on the opinions of the supportive people in your life who care about you and know how awesome you are.

Fight Back without Fighting

Most bullying doesn't start out as physical aggression, but some situations can get out of control. It's important to know how to respond without choosing violence. Take Blake, for example:

Kenneth and Blake were friends last year in fourth grade. For some reason, this year, Kenneth seems to really have a problem with Blake. He has been bothering Blake on the bus for several weeks now. Each week, his actions toward Blake have gotten worse. One day on the bus, he keeps insulting Blake over and over, but Blake doesn't respond at all, which makes Kenneth furious. When they arrive at their bus stop and get off, Kenneth throws his backpack to the ground, walks up to Blake, and gets right in his face, ready to fight. Blake looks Kenneth in the eye and says, "Dude! What are you so upset about? We used to be friends and now you're trying to fight me? Can we at least talk about this?" Kenneth steps back and looks at Blake. Finally, he reminds Blake about a situation that happened in fourth grade that he's never forgotten about. Blake says, "Man . . . I'm sorry. I didn't realize how much that upset you, but we don't have to fight about it. Let's talk." Kenneth backs off. He doesn't really feel like talking about it in that moment, but he decides against fighting Blake.

One important part of Blake's plan was that he made sure he remained calm and showed confidence by looking Kenneth in the eye. He didn't return anger toward Kenneth. He admitted that he upset Kenneth in the past, and he tried to talk with him about it. Although Kenneth didn't want to talk, Blake was able to stop the situation from getting out of hand.

A plan can help you avoid physical violence so that no one gets hurt.

QUICK TIP: Karate and other martial arts classes can help you build confidence and stand taller. When you carry yourself with confidence, you become a less likely target.

Defending Yourself

If you are ever in a situation where you feel like you might get hurt, and you can't run away, get to an adult, or get the bully to back off, the only option may be to defend yourself. Physically defending yourself is different from fighting— nobody should just stand there and get punched or assaulted in any way. However, defending yourself physically should be a last resort when all other strategies have been attempted and the pros and cons have been considered. Cons: If you fight, someone will most likely get hurt. If you don't defend yourself and someone is attacking you, though, you will *definitely* get hurt. Pros: Once you defend yourself, the person might not bother you anymore. Also, if you defend yourself, you may avoid getting hurt.

If you find yourself in this kind of situation, be sure to report your experience to an adult. Adults can be on the look-out for bullying behaviors so it's less likely the bully will target someone else in the future.

GET HELP WHEN YOU NEED IT

If you find yourself in a bullying situation, always remember you are not alone. Children have adults in their lives for a good reason. Call on your trusted adults, as well as good friends, to support you when you need help.

WHEN SHOULD I ASK FOR HELP?

Having a plan to stand up for yourself is great, but when a situation gets out of control, seek help from an adult. Here are some warning signs:

- Someone hurts you.

- Someone threatens you.

- Someone takes your belongings.

- Someone destroys your property.

- Someone uses hate speech against your race, religion, gender, sexual orientation, or any other part of your identity.

- Someone hacks or uses your online identity.

- You feel physically sick and want to skip school.

- You have trouble sleeping from worry and stress.

- Your grades are going down because of your worries.

- You've tried standing up for yourself, but the bully won't stop.

If you experience any of these warning signs, ask for help right away. Don't suffer alone. There are people who can help.

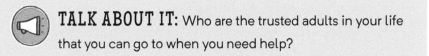

TALK ABOUT IT: Who are the trusted adults in your life that you can go to when you need help?

LEAN ON YOUR FRIENDS

It's okay to ask a friend or another kid for help. Here are some ideas for how they can help you:

- Ask a friend to sit with you during lunchtime.

- Meet up with a friend during recess so you are not alone.

- Find someone who can walk with you on the way home from the bus stop.

- Ask a friend to come with you as support when you report the bully.

- Ask a friend to stand with you while you stand up to the bully.

What if you feel like you don't have any friends who can help? If this is the case, try connecting with other kids you've seen in the same situation as you. It's very likely that the same person bullying you is bullying others, too. Even if they are dealing with a different bully, show empathy to others and let them know you understand what they are going through. You can also do simple acts of kindness for others, like helping someone with math, sharing a pencil, or just picking something up from the floor for the person who dropped it. As you show kindness toward others, they will remember your good character and hopefully make an effort to help you if you need them. And by helping others, you will build up your own self-confidence.

STANDING TOGETHER

Here are two examples of how adults and friends can stand with you and support you in a bullying situation:

Ronnie wishes Todd would leave him alone. He doesn't want to go back to school. Ronnie talks with his dad about it. That night, he and his dad practice what he could say by role-playing. His dad pretends to be Todd, and after a couple of tries, Ronnie feels like he's ready to stand up for himself. The next day, Todd hurls his usual insults at Ronnie. Todd is surprised when Ronnie doesn't get upset and instead stands up for himself. It isn't long before the insults stop. It is almost like Todd isn't even there anymore.

How did the role-playing help Ronnie? Why do you think Todd stopped insulting him?

After getting a third disrespectful e-mail from Jamie, Amber tells her friend Victoria about it. Victoria knows Jamie very well, so she asks Amber to print the e-mail and bring it to school the next day. At school, Victoria shows the e-mail to Jamie and says, "I hope this is the last e-mail you'll send to Amber like this one. It's not nice to treat others this way. I wonder if Mrs. Richards would like to see it." Jamie's eyes get big for a second. Then she says, "It was just a joke. It won't happen again."

How did Victoria's actions make things better for Amber?

HELP OTHERS

It's important to keep yourself bully-free, but it's also good to be ready to help others. Next, we'll explore how you can use your words and actions to help when others are being bullied.

WATCH OUT FOR BULLYING

One of the first ways you can help is by learning how to recognize kids who are being bullied. Unless you see the bullying for yourself, it's not always easy to recognize. However, if you know someone well enough, or are around a person regularly, you may be able to figure it out.

Here are 10 signs you might see from people who are being bullied:

1. They appear sad or down more often than usual.

2. They miss several days of school.

3. They seem nervous most of the time.

4. They appear upset at times but won't talk about it.

5. They avoid activities they used to love.

6. They have angry outbursts.

7. They may not hang out with friends like before.

8. They act differently and aren't their usual selves.

9. They begin to put themselves down.

10. You hear them saying, "I hate my life."

Now let's talk about some ways you can help.

 QUICK TIP: If you ever hear someone say "I hate my life" or a similar statement, be sure to let an adult know as soon as you can. Kids who feel this low need support right away.

HELP WITH WORDS

Defend Your Friend

A person who witnesses bullying is called a *bystander*. As a bystander, you have two choices:

1. Do nothing.

2. Become an *upstander* by standing up for the target.

Hopefully, you will choose to stand up and be an upstander, rather than just a bystander! If you feel safe, you can speak up and defend the target. You don't have to say too much to get your point across. Let's look at two examples, along with what you could say in each situation:

When checking your e-mail, you see a message from LaToya and notice it has been sent to three of your other friends, too. This e-mail makes fun of a new student named Adeelah, who wears a hijab (a headscarf) because of her religious beliefs. You have gotten to know Adeelah for the past two weeks, and this e-mail was not funny to you at all.

You could reply:

- "Please don't e-mail mean jokes like this to me again."
- "Adeelah is pretty cool. Maybe you should learn about why she wears it."
- "I wonder what our teacher will think about this."

Derek is a student with special needs in your class. He usually likes to be alone and has a hard time being around a lot of kids. You've noticed your classmate Craig often teases him and does things to make Derek irritated. Today, in the locker room after gym class, you hear Craig and a friend of his making rude comments and laughing at Derek. Derek covers his ears and turns away.

You could reply:

- "Cut it out, Craig!"
- "You bother him every day. Stop being a bully!"
- "Leave him alone, or I'll tell the coach."

Just like when you stand up for yourself with words, using your words to help others is a powerful tool that will make bullies think twice. It will also show targets of bullying that you recognize what is happening, you understand how the situation makes them feel, and you are on their side.

TALK ABOUT IT: When might be a time that you, as a bystander, should NOT stand up to a bully, and instead get help from an adult?

REAL-LIFE STORY

Monica is so glad that Angela has stopped bothering her. It happened for so long, but it has finally stopped. However, it looks like Angela has found someone else to pick on. Tuan is a new student in their class. She is very nice and makes friends easily. Angela is jealous and now does everything she can to lower Tuan's spirits. Monica has listened each day as Angela laughs at Tuan's outfits, telling her she needs to go back home and change. She has also heard Angela tell Tuan that no one really likes her, and she should go back to the school she came from. Monica feels bad for Tuan. One day in class, Angela sees Tuan's tablet on the right side of her desk. As she walks past, she purposely bumps into Tuan's desk, knocking the tablet to the floor. Tuan quickly picks her device up off the floor and tries to turn it on, but the screen remains black. Monica sees everything and knows that Angela broke it on purpose. Angela tells the teacher it was an accident, all the while laughing under her breath at Tuan. Monica shakes her head in disbelief. How can Angela keep getting away with this?

LET'S DISCUSS: How could Monica have helped or stood up for Tuan in each situation?

When to Tell

If you are a bystander to bullying and you don't feel safe enough to stand up to the bully, it's important to tell an adult. Telling an adult about a bully is not tattling, or what some kids call "snitching." There is a big difference between tattling and telling. Kids who tattle are usually trying to get another person in trouble for things that aren't hurting anyone. When you tell an adult about bullying, you are helping keep someone safe and out of trouble. So in this case, it's super important to speak up in order to help.

Many kids don't tell an adult about bullying situations because they are afraid of retaliation, or the bully "getting even" with them. It is really important to bring any bullying situations out into the open and tell a trusted adult, so parents and school officials can do their part to make sure the bullying doesn't occur again and that everyone gets the help they need.

YOUR CALL:
IS IT TATTLING OR TELLING?

Each of the following statements tells a story. In each case, would reporting what you witnessed be tattling or telling? Why?

Remember, **tattling** is getting others *in* trouble and **telling** is helping keep others *safe* and *out of trouble*.

1. I saw Jerome tear the strap on Lori's bag.

2. Luis kept making faces at Jessica instead of doing his work.

3. I heard Rhonda tell Tina she didn't like her coat.

4. James said he's going to punch Stuart after school.

5. During recess, André pushed Davon really hard and made him fall to the ground.

6. Maggie rolled her eyes when Keisha walked past her desk.

7. Nyla scratched Isabella on the arm because she wouldn't give her the ball.

8. I saw William take a classmate's cell phone and slip it into his backpack.

9. John refused to pick Renée to be on his team for kickball.

10. At lunch, Melody showed us a cigarette lighter that was hidden in her lunch box.

(Turn the page for answers.)

ANSWERS

1. Telling: Jerome is damaging Lori's property.

2. Tattling: Luis is not hurting Jessica by making faces at her.

3. Tattling: It wasn't nice of her to say, but Rhonda is not hurting Tina.

4. Telling: Stuart could get hurt and an adult needs to know.

5. Telling: Davon was pushed to the ground and could have been hurt.

6. Tattling: Maggie isn't hurting Keisha by rolling her eyes at her.

7. Telling: Nyla hurt Isabella by scratching her.

8. Telling: William is stealing something from someone.

9. Tattling: John did not hurt Renée, although she may be upset about not being picked.

10. Telling: A cigarette lighter can cause a fire and many people could be hurt.

Show Support

We have talked about the difference between being a bystander and an upstander. It is very helpful to targets of bullying to feel supported by others. This support will encourage them and help build their confidence. Here are five things you can say to someone who is being bullied to show support:

1. "I'm sorry she is being so mean to you."

2. "That's happened to me before. Do you want to talk?"

3. "We'd love for you to eat lunch with us."

4. "I disagree with how he is treating you."

5. "Let's stick together so you're not alone."

Supportive words and actions can really mean a lot to bullying targets. It can be a lifeline to that person to realize they are not alone and that someone cares.

HELP WITH ACTIONS

Another way to help others is through your actions. As an upstander, you can help create an environment where kids who may be bullying targets can feel supported.

Be respectful. Think about how you would want to be treated, and treat others that way. If you see someone who needs help, reach out and help if you can.

Show kindness and consideration. Say hello or ask "How are you doing?" Give a friendly smile or wave to let others know you see them in a positive light. Make an effort to avoid saying or doing things that may make others feel bad.

Be accepting. Throughout your lifetime, you will have the chance to meet people from different places and different backgrounds. Some people may look different or behave differently from you because of special needs or circumstances. They may even speak a different language from you. Take the time to get to know and understand them. If there are things you don't understand, ask questions and learn.

Show compassion. When you see others having a hard time, show that you are concerned about them and what they are going through. It can mean a lot to others when someone takes the time to reach out and show they care.

Be inclusive. Many targets of bullying are left out on purpose, and they feel sad and alone. Be the one who invites new students and friends to play, hang out, or eat lunch with you. Try your best to be aware of kids who are alone but may not really want to be alone. An invitation to join you and your friends will mean the world to those people.

Show courage. Be the one who others know will always stand up for what's right. Don't become a part of the bully's audience. Instead, be the one who encourages others to take a stand—be an upstander.

HELP A BULLY

What? Yes, believe it or not, even kids who bully need help. Let's think back to the reasons why some kids bully (see Why Do Kids Bully?, page 3). This time we'll focus on strategies you can try in order to deal with the bully's behavior. By using these strategies, you could possibly even see a change in the bully. It's definitely worth a try.

REASON KIDS BULLY: LEARNED BEHAVIOR

Possible strategy: Try pointing out the person's kind and respectful deeds toward others. Say things like "That was nice of you to let Emily use your pencil," or "What you said about Reggie's new shoes was really nice." You can also be a good example of showing kindness and respect. Doing this may give the person a desire to learn more positive behaviors, and hopefully he or she will begin to show them as well.

REASON KIDS BULLY: POWER AND CONTROL

Possible strategy: A person who likes having power and control needs to be encouraged to use their power in a positive way. As they begin to make better choices, and with supervision, you might consider calling on them to help you care for a pet or a younger sibling. At school, ask your teacher if you and the person can read to younger students. Whatever that power is, help the person use it for something good. Soon, these kids may realize that being their true selves is good enough, and they won't need to use power and control to get what they want.

REASON KIDS BULLY: LACK OF EMPATHY

Possible strategy: Try showing empathy toward the person if you have the chance. You can also make an effort to reach out to him or her as a friend. You might be surprised, but that small gesture may be just what that person needs to begin showing empathy, too.

REASON KIDS BULLY: LOW SELF-CONCEPT

Possible strategy: Many bullies feel like no one really cares or even notices them, which is why many seek so much attention with their actions. Try finding opportunities to point out the bully's positive qualities and strengths. Doing so may help the person focus on those areas more and focus less on bringing others down.

REASON KIDS BULLY: IGNORANCE ABOUT DIFFERENCES

Possible strategy: Try giving the person opportunities to learn about and get to know people who are different from him or her. Encourage the person to ask questions so he or she can understand more about unfamiliar cultures, religions, or ways of life. Maybe you can point out opportunities, such as "Hey, that new kid Johnny is teaching me his language. Do you want to learn?" or "Frankie is awesome at chess. You should see him." With time, the person will hopefully begin to appreciate those differences.

Bullies don't have to stay bullies, and you can play a part in making a difference. However, remember that you can't change anyone who doesn't want to. The person has to want to change. Hopefully, your actions will encourage him or her to do just that.

DEFEAT CYBERBULLIES

In order to defeat cyberbullies, it's important to protect yourself, stand up for cyberbullying targets, and be kind online. Here are some tips to remember:

1. Never, ever share your e-mail or social media account passwords—not even with your BFF. If a password gets in the wrong hands, that person can post anything online, and it will look just like it came from you.

2. Don't respond to hateful e-mails and text messages. However, do keep them as evidence to show an adult. Print, save, or take a screenshot.

3. Block the bully's account username or e-mail address so he or she is unable to contact you again.

4. Don't share your personal information on gaming or social media sites.

5. Ignore messages or e-mails from usernames and e-mail addresses you don't recognize.

6. Never leave your accounts open for easy access. Protect your device with a passcode and log out of your accounts when you are finished. Use a different password for each account.

7. Don't post embarrassing pictures of yourself. They may be just for fun on your page, but remember that anyone can copy or screenshot your pictures and do whatever they want with them.

8. Even though you may feel angry or upset, don't bully back—this will only make the situation worse and pull you into the blame.

9. If someone sends you a mean message or embarrassing picture of someone else, don't participate in the bullying by forwarding or reposting. This kind of participation shows approval of the bully's actions. Tell an adult who can take charge of the situation.

10. Before you post anything online or click Send on an e-mail, think about it. Ask yourself: *Will I feel good about people seeing this? Will the person that my post or e-mail is about feel good seeing this?* If there are any doubts, do not post it.

11. Never post anything offensive or embarrassing to someone else online.

12. If you are being bullied online or know of someone else who is, do not wait! Tell an adult right away and get help.

13. If you ever see acts of cyberbullying on social media or anywhere online, you can show support by sending kind notes or flooding the target's profile with kind posts of support.

14. It's okay to decide that you aren't going to be on social media. Simply avoiding that whole situation can keep you safe from a lot of unnecessary drama.

QUICK TIP: Remember, when you're online and you click Send, your post or message can go wherever the receiver wants it to go. Never send messages that you don't want others to see. Be smart and thoughtful about what you share on the Internet.

THREE

Become Bully-Proof

WHAT IS RESILIENCE?

Resilience is a big word, but it's not that difficult to understand. Imagine a large, beautiful palm tree in the middle of a hurricane. The winds blow and blow, and the tree bends over so far it almost touches the ground. Once the storm moves away, that very same tree is standing straight up again and ready to face another day. That's resilience.

Resilience is the ability to bounce back, or recover, after you have faced a big challenge.

Can you remember a time when you were faced with a challenge and you had a hard time dealing with it? Maybe someone said something very hurtful to you, or maybe someone you trusted really disappointed you. These are times when resilience can help you.

QUICK TIP: As you begin increasing your resilience, always remember to believe in yourself. You can handle the challenges that come your way, and you have people who can help support you and who believe in you, too.

Resilience is:

- having an embarrassing moment at school, but returning the next day with your head up.

- showing perseverance—that is, continuing to try when things are hard for you.

- realizing that you've made it through difficult times.

- not making the team, but still practicing all year until the next tryouts.

- realizing that just because a bully says something about you that doesn't make it true.

Instead of letting a situation get you down, it's so much better for you to learn from it. Challenges will come—they are just a part of life. However, with resilience, you will be more prepared to face those challenges head on and keep moving forward with your chin up.

You can do things to increase your resilience so you won't feel helpless when it comes to dealing with bullying behavior. The following sections will give you suggestions for increasing your resilience. As you continue reading, think about how these ideas can help you on your way to becoming bully-proof.

STAY POSITIVE

Although we don't have control over everything in life, there are some things we can control. Having a positive attitude is one of those things. Sometimes we spend too much energy focused on what went wrong or on things that aren't going as planned. Whether you are dealing with bullying, helping someone else through a tough time, or just handling a problem in your own life, keeping a positive attitude will give you a better outlook.

Here are some ideas to keep yourself feeling and thinking positively:

Positive self-talk: Positive self-talk is when you think and say positive things about yourself. *I am awesome. I am talented. I am kind. I am artistic. My sister thinks I am the greatest.* This is a good exercise to use when you are dealing with a bully, especially when the bully is saying negative things about you. Remind yourself of your positive qualities and all the things that make you the wonderful person you are. Positive self-talk is also very useful when you make mistakes or are unsuccessful at something you've tried to do. Tell yourself to keep trying and that you will get better. Say "I can totally do this!" before getting ready to face a challenge. Positive self-talk can help build your confidence and will remind you that you can make it through difficult times.

Gratitude journal: A gratitude journal is great for helping you stay focused on the positive things in your life. What or who are you thankful for? What is something good that happened today? *I got an A on my test. My neighbor wants me to babysit. My dog loves to play with me. I made a new friend today.* When you take the time to focus on things that are going well and think about what makes you feel grateful, you can become more prepared to deal with roadblocks during challenging times. Instead of being overwhelmed with what may be going wrong, you will have something to look at to remind you of what is going right.

Positive affirmations: Positive affirmations are statements you read each day to give yourself encouragement. These are especially good for areas where you need support. You can think up your own positive affirmations, write them on small pieces of paper, and put them in places where you will see them each day as reminders. *I have the courage to stand up to anyone. I am an awesome person who is going to do great things. I am kind to everyone.* Repeat your affirmations each day, believe them, and live by them.

TALK ABOUT IT: What are some positive affirmations you can focus on and read daily? Think of two or three things you want to remind yourself of, write them on index cards or sticky notes, and put them someplace where you can read them every day.

FOLLOW YOUR INTERESTS
(OR TRY SOMETHING NEW!)

Most people have activities they are interested in or hobbies they enjoy doing. When you discover the things you really enjoy, it's great to find ways to make those activities a part of your regular routine. That will give you something positive to look forward to and will make you feel great inside. As a bonus, it will also create opportunities for you to make new friends.

Here are a few tips for getting involved in positive activities:

- If you have a sport you are interested in and want to learn, take lessons or join a local team. You may have friends who already belong to a team. Ask a parent or guardian if you can attend a practice to see if it's a good fit for you and, if it is, try out for the team.

- If the arts are something you really enjoy doing, think about joining a club at your school. Many schools have a chorus or other musical clubs you could be a part of. There may be art, writing, or dance clubs you could join. Ask a parent or guardian to sign you up for arts activities in your town or city.

- Martial arts, such as karate, are not just good for physical self-defense. These can help you build confidence and stand taller, making you less likely to be a target of bullying.

- Scouting (like Boy Scouts or Girl Scouts) is another positive activity in which you can learn new skills, make friends, and go camping. Every new experience you seek will allow your list of interests to grow, creating even more opportunities for fun activities.

Whatever it is you enjoy doing, find opportunities to do that activity so you can spend time with others who have a common interest. Think about what you really enjoy or would like to learn, and find a way to do that activity on a regular basis. Regularly taking part in things you enjoy will make you feel good on the inside, and your positive attitude and resilience will continue to grow stronger.

 TALK ABOUT IT: What are some activities that you would enjoy doing regularly? How would they benefit you?

KEEP YOUR COOL

Knowing how to keep your cool when you come face-to-face with a difficult situation is important. You don't want to fall apart every time you are faced with a challenge. You also want to be ready if you find yourself having to deal with a bully. Here are a few strategies you can use to help yourself stay calm and lower your stress after an incident:

Breathe deep. Focused breathing is a great way to calm your mind and body. Close your eyes and put your hands on your stomach. Slowly breathe in through your nose and count to three in your head during that breath. Hold the breath for a second or two, and then breathe the air out slowly through your mouth. While breathing, notice your hands moving down and up.

Be still. Find a quiet place in your home or outside at school. Sit quietly and close your eyes. What sounds do you notice? You might hear the cough of a parent, the voice of a classmate, the rustling of trees, or even a motorcycle driving by. Stay focused only on the sounds you hear as you clear your mind of anything causing you stress.

Relax your body. Sit in a chair that has a back. Start by focusing on your toes. Think about how they feel. Wiggle them. Pretend to make a fist with them and hold it for a few seconds before letting go and relaxing. Do the same with other parts of your body, like your legs, shoulders, arms, hands, and even your face. Each time you focus on a body part, be sure to end by squeezing and focusing your energy into that part of your body before relaxing it.

When you use strategies like these, you can help position yourself to think clearly and make better decisions. You will realize that you are okay, and then you can take the next steps to handle the situation.

> **QUICK TIP:** Listen to your body. When you feel the signs of stress in your body (fast heartbeat, tight shoulders, sweaty palms, nervous stomach) it's a good time to use one of your strategies that will help you feel relaxed and calm down.

LEARN PROBLEM SOLVING

Whenever you are faced with a challenge, your goal should be to figure out how to make things better. Some problems can be solved easily, but sometimes you may need to take several steps to find the best solution. The following steps can help you be your own problem solver:

1. **Identify your problem.** What is the problem, and why? How is it affecting you?

2. **Brainstorm.** Come up with different strategies or ideas to try to solve the problem. Some of your ideas may not work, so it's important to come up with several.

3. **Weigh pros and cons.** Consider the pros: what is good about each strategy; and cons: what is not so good. If you find an idea with lots of cons, you may want to cut that one from your list. When you have more pros than cons, that idea is likely to be a better choice.

4. **Choose a strategy.** After weighing the pros and cons for each idea, choose the one you think will get the best results and try it.

5. **Evaluate.** Once you've tried one of your strategies, ask yourself: *Did it work? Is my problem fixed or at least better?* If your strategy worked and your problem has gotten better or is solved, great! Mission accomplished! However, if you tried a strategy and the problem doesn't seem to be getting any better, try a new strategy from your list and start again.

With a problem-solving plan in your hand, you will be more confident in your ability to handle different situations, and you are less likely to feel helpless. And guess what? When you aren't helpless, you are more resilient. Tougher. Amazing!

QUICK TIP: If your problem doesn't involve you or someone else getting hurt or threatened, use the problem-solving steps. Otherwise, tell a trusted adult so they can help.

REAL-LIFE STORY

Like most kids, Ray likes getting extra snacks when he goes through the lunch line each day at school. He often buys his favorite chips, an ice cream sandwich, or a cookie. He likes to find a spot alone to read and enjoy his lunch. Edgar is a little older and bigger than Ray. Edgar will often take Ray's snack, without worrying that Ray will ever do anything about it. One day Edgar takes Ray's sugar cookie, and Ray, who wants this bullying to stop, decides to problem-solve. He thinks about two ways to solve his problem. His first idea is to sit in a different location with his friend Terry in hopes that Edgar will leave him alone. He thinks this might work because it's possible that Edgar won't bother him if he isn't alone. Also, Terry could stand up for Ray. Ray thinks it might not work, though, because Edgar might not care that Terry is there and will take his snack anyway. His second idea is to just stand up to Edgar, and Edgar will realize he can't get what he wants from Ray. On the other hand, Edgar might actually hurt Ray to get what he wants.

LET'S DISCUSS: Which of the two solutions should Ray choose and why?

FOCUS ON THE FUTURE

You won't always be a kid. One day, the things you are dealing with now will be distant memories. However, this doesn't mean you'll ever forget your experiences, and that's really okay. Our experiences often give us wisdom and help us grow stronger. Hopefully you will use your experiences and everything you've learned to help someone else.

You have so many things to look forward to in life. Growing up isn't always easy, but as you build resilience, you will be able to make it through difficult times more easily, so you can look ahead at what's to come with a can-do attitude. Have you ever thought about your future?

- It may seem like a long time from now, but one day you will graduate from high school. Everything you are doing right now is preparing you for that exciting time. You are going to be so proud of yourself, and it will be a very big accomplishment.

- After you graduate from high school, you will get to choose what you want to do for work. You might already have an idea of what you'd like to be when you grow up. When that time comes, you will get to follow the path that leads you there, whether it's college, trade school, joining the military, or starting your own business.

- Don't wait—start preparing for your future path! For example, if you like photography, enter your photographs in a contest or the state fair. If you want to learn a trade or specialized skill, see if your county has a technical high school you can visit to learn more. This can make you feel good about your future and take the focus off what might be stressing you out today.

- Once you have a job, you'll be able to take care of yourself and can live on your own. When you get to that place in your life, you will be ready to make decisions for yourself.

- The past will be the past. You will look back on your child- hood. Were you an upstander? Were you kind to others? Did you stand tall with confidence? Did you get through tough times with resilience? You will get to look at your past and decide how you can use your skills to help others moving forward. As for those who were kind and those who were maybe not so kind, they will all look back, too. If you are true to yourself, you will always be proud of who you are.

As you continue to learn and grow, just stay focused on what's to come. When times get tough, celebrate each accomplishment—even the little ones—because they are getting you one step closer to your future goals. Remind yourself that problems, although sometimes tough, are temporary. They will not last, and they will make you stronger. The resilience you are growing now will help you so much in the future—who knows? Maybe one day you will be a counselor or leader who helps others!

YOUR CALL:
SHOWING RESILIENCE

Read each scenario and decide the best way to show resilience from the choices that follow.

SCENARIO 1

Donovan is so excited about his YouTube channel. He posts videos every weekend telling his followers how to beat different levels in popular video games. His follower list is growing every week, and he likes answering their questions and reading their great feedback in the comment sections. One day, WonderChick, a new follower, leaves a not-so-rave review. In fact, WonderChick writes that his videos suck and that Donovan should get off YouTube. This makes Donovan upset, but he decides to ignore WonderChick. Over the next few days, he notices thumbs-down icons popping up on all of his videos and more negative feedback from WonderChick. He gets so frustrated, he can feel his heart racing and he wants to throw his tablet across the room.

Donovan has learned all the strategies you've read about in this chapter. From the following choices, which would be the best strategy for him to use in order to show his resilience, and why?

a) Follow Your Interests
b) Keep Your Cool
c) Focus on the Future

Itzel is one of the newest members on her soccer team. She never misses a practice and always gives her best at each game. She isn't a starter and knows she has to make lots of improvements before she will be able to get more time on the field. A few of the girls on the team often give her a hard time about her skills. They give her disappointed looks when she fails to make an "easy" goal. She often sees them huddled together after practice looking over at her. She just knows they must be talking about her. She begins to feel like quitting the team.

Itzel has also learned all the strategies you've read about in this chapter. From the following choices, which would be the best strategy for her to use in order to show her resilience, and why?

a) Stay Positive
b) Focus on the Future
c) Learn Problem-Solving

ANSWERS

b) Keep Your Cool. Although Donovan is feeling very angry about the comments and the thumbs-down being left on his YouTube channel, he should focus on remaining calm so he is able to think about ways to solve his problem.

a) Stay Positive. Itzel should avoid telling herself that she's not good enough for the team. She should focus on her positive qualities and use positive self-talk instead of making a plan to quit the team.

MAKE A PACT

A pact is an agreement that people make with one another. You can make a pact about anything! You can make a pact with your brother not to take each other's favorite snack out of the pantry, or you can make a pact with a friend to participate together in the school talent show. Once you make the agreement, you need to do your absolute best to keep your promise. Just imagine what could happen if everyone made a pact to help end bullying!

Here's a pact you can use with a friend, a group, your class, or even your entire school:

1. We promise to treat everyone with kindness and respect.

2. We promise to stand up for people who are being bullied when we see it or suspect it.

3. We promise to stick together and include people who are purposely being left out.

4. We promise to talk with trusted adults about bullying when it happens—whether it's happening to us or someone else.

5. We promise to accept, appreciate, and learn from other people's differences.

6. We promise to take notice of warning signs of bullying so we can stop it quickly.

7. We promise to show support for targets of bullying through positive messages.

8. We promise to keep mean and hurtful online messages from spreading.

9. We promise to fight back without fighting.

10. We promise to encourage others to take a stand against bullying.

Here's another great idea: Make a signature page to go along with your pact. Everyone who agrees to the pact signs his or her name. Display your pact where everyone can see it, and keep a copy of your pact in a safe place.

Is it possible to become bully-proof? Yes, it is! When everyone comes together and takes a stand against bullying, things will begin to change for the better. What will you do to help put a stop to bullying? Always remember to stand tall and proud—you've got what it takes!

 TALK ABOUT IT: Who are some friends you would like to make this pact with? Is there anything else you would add to it?

RESOURCES

There are so many great sources of advice and additional information about bullying in print and on the Internet. The following are just a few book titles and websites that you can check out for more information about bullying.

BOOKS AND WEBSITES FOR KIDS

Many great books geared for kids focus on the topic of bullying. The following books go along perfectly with the information in this book. Some of these books are informational, and the others tell fictional stories of kids in different situations and what they did to solve their problems. There's even one book that comes from the side of a bully.

- Fox, Debbie, and Allan L. Beane. *Good-Bye Bully Machine*. Minneapolis, MN: Free Spirit Publishing, 2009.
- Ludwig, Trudy. *Confessions of a Former Bully*. Berkeley, CA: Tricycle Press, 2009.
- Romain, Trevor. *Bullies Are a Pain in the Brain*, rev. ed. Minneapolis, MN: Free Spirit Publishing, 2016.

- Sornson, Bob. *It's Time to Stand Up and Speak Up! For Yourself and Others.* Northville, MI: Ferne Press, 2013.
- Sornson, Bob, and Maria Dismondy. *The Juice Box Bully: Empowering Kids to Stand Up for Others.* Northville, MI: Ferne Press, 2010.
- Sornson, Bob. *Stand in My Shoes: Kids Learning about Empathy.* Golden, CO: Love and Logic Press, 2013.

WEBSITES

The following websites explore what you've read about in this book. Some feature videos that focus on being safe on the Internet and interview kids about different bullying situations. These sites also talk about ways you can help in the fight against bullying.

- NetSmartzKids.org
- PACERKidsAgainstBullying.org
- STOMPOutBullying.org
- StopBullying.gov/kids/what-you-can-do

CALL CENTERS

Although it's always best to tell a trusted adult if you need help, these are some places you can call when you need somewhere safe to turn.

- Bullying Advocacy 24/7 call center (located in California): (844) 256-0735
- Loveisrespect 24/7 hotline: (866) 331-9474
- National Suicide Prevention Lifeline: (800) 273-8255

BOOKS AND WEBSITES FOR ADULTS

Parents, teachers, and other adults who care about you can check out the following books and websites. Some of these websites are also useful to kids.

Books

- Borba, Michele. *UnSelfie*. New York: Touchstone, 2016.
- Colorosa, Barbara. *The Bully, the Bullied, and the Bystander*, updated. New York: Collins Living, 2009.
- Thomas, Jason. *Parent's Guide to Preventing and Responding to Bullying*. North Charleston, SC: CreateSpace Independent Publishing, 2011.

Websites

- AccreditedSchoolsOnline.org/resources /lgbtq-student-support
- CDC.gov/lgbthealth/youth-resources.htm
- CyberBullyHelp.com
- Cyberbullying.org
- EyesOnBullying.org
- Pacer.org/bullying
- NetFamilyNews.org
- NoBullying.com
- StopBullying.gov
- TogetherAgainstBullying.org

INDEX

ACKNOWLEDGMENTS

To Katie and the Callisto Media team . . . I'm thankful for the opportunity to author my first book with such an organized and professional group of people. I'm forever grateful that you chose me to be the voice to help young children navigate through the topic of bullying. Thank you!

To my daughter, Domonique, my father, Eddie Green, and my entire family, of which there are too many names to call out without getting myself into trouble . . . Thank you for your love and your continued support throughout my journey.

To Gerrelyn and Felissa . . . Thank you for sharing your writing expertise with me over the years and for helping me to get to a place where I could actually be ready to do this. Words can't express how much I appreciate you.

To Sharon, Tara, Valerie, Rhesia, and Lindsey . . . Thank you for helping me when I needed to brainstorm and for allowing me to bounce my ideas back and forth with you. I really appreciate it!

ABOUT THE AUTHOR

 **VANESSA GREEN ALLEN** is a professional school counselor living in Raleigh, North Carolina. As a counselor, she regularly teaches her students about the effects of bullying and shares strategies with them in classroom lessons, small group sessions, and individually. She received her bachelor of arts degree in elementary education from North Carolina Central University and her master of education degree in counseling from North Carolina State University. Vanessa is a former second-grade teacher, and she has worked for the Wake County Public School System since 1991. She is a 2009 National Board Certified teacher in the area of school counseling. Vanessa is also the creator and author of SavvySchoolCounselor.com, where she shares ideas and resources with school counselors across the globe.

UNOFFICIAL GUIDE TO
ANCESTRY
.COM